IMAGES
of America

PHILLIPSBURG

On the far left of this c. 1910 picture of Union Square is the Lee House, later known as the Wardell Hotel. The Union Square Hotel, erected in 1811, is in the center, and on the far right are the Phillipsburg National Bank and the Pennsylvania Railroad passenger station. The station was demolished in 1949, the bank c. 1930. The Wardell Hotel was destroyed by fire in January 1967. The area at the top of the hill is known as Mount Lebanon.

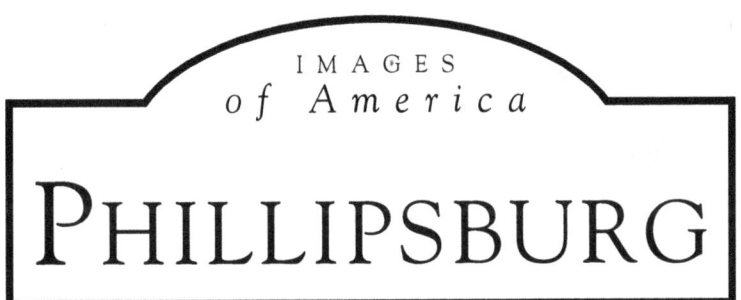

Images of America
Phillipsburg

Dr. Leonard Buscemi Sr.

Copyright © 2001 by Dr. Leonard Buscemi Sr.
ISBN 978-1-5316-0574-2

Published by Arcadia Publishing
Charleston, South Carolina

Library of Congress Catalog Card Number: 2001091400

For all general information contact Arcadia Publishing at:
Telephone 843-853-2070
Fax 843-853-0044
E-mail sales@arcadiapublishing.com
For customer service and orders:
Toll-Free 1-888-313-2665

Visit us on the Internet at www.arcadiapublishing.com

CONTENTS

Introduction		7
1.	A Religious Community	11
2.	School Days	23
3.	Industry	37
4.	Public Service	49
5.	Medical Care	65
6.	Local Merchants	75
7.	Recreation and Sports	89
8.	Transportation	99
9.	Disasters	109
10.	Views about Town	119
Acknowledgments		128

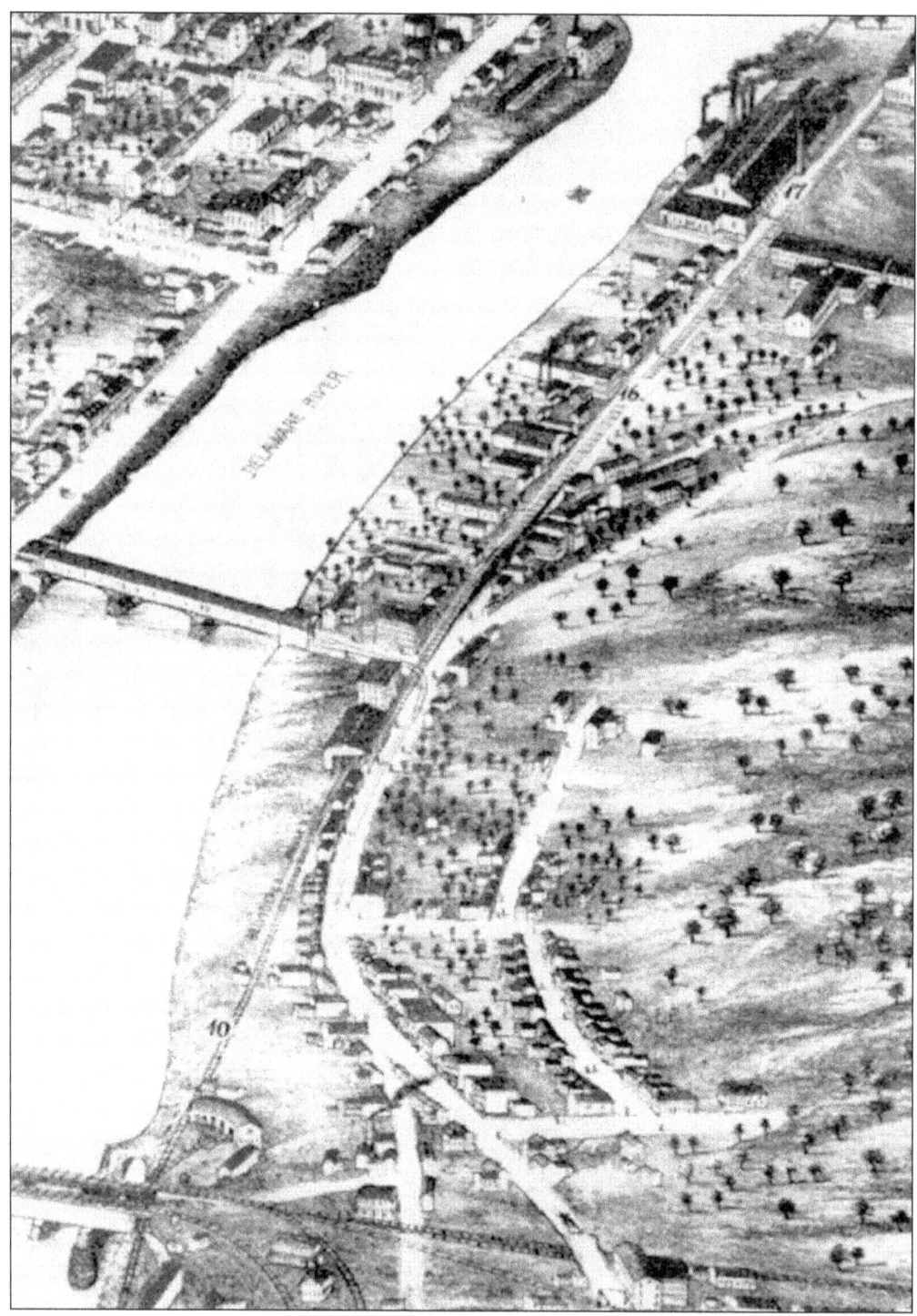

Most dwellings, stores, and industry were located in an area known as the Flats, along the Delaware River, as shown in this 1873 image. Some homes were built on the hill section as early as 1853. The covered bridge to Easton was replaced in 1895–1896 by the present day Free Bridge.

Introduction

The largest town in Warren County is located on the banks of the Delaware River. Its high elevation provides Phillipsburg a most commanding appearance. In 1654, the area that comprises the present site of the town, according to a map made by Dutch engineer Adrian Vonder Donk, was a Native American settlement called Chinktewink. The common Native American custom was to clear the land around the village for raising corn, which was done in the area now known as the Flats.

There is controversy over the origin of the name Phillipsburg. One belief is that the town was named after an old Native American chief named Phillip. Another is that the town was named after a large landowner by the name of Phillips. However, the name Phillipsburg was used on a map of the inhabited parts of Pennsylvania and New Jersey published by Evans in 1749, and this was before landowner Phillips resided here.

On November 24, 1755, Native Americans raided Gnadenhutten, Pennsylvania. A panic ensued, and all Native Americans were then considered unfriendly. The Native American Chief Phillip was an intimate friend of the great Chief Teedyuscung. Chief Phillip and 14 other Native Americans were arrested in December 1775 and were committed to prison in Easton, Pennsylvania, which had the only jailhouse in the area.

In 1752, a Philadelphia merchant named Cox, who owned about 411 acres along the Old Fields or Flats, contemplated laying out a town. His intent alarmed the proprietors of Pennsylvania, who were fearful that a town across the Delaware River would hinder the infant town of Easton. In a May 9, 1752 letter to Richard Peters, Thomas Penn wrote, "I think we should secure all the land we can on the Jersey Side of the water." The intention was to retain the land and prevent the development of a town.

Cox abandoned his project of laying out a town on the New Jersey side. Cox's land was sold at a sheriff's sale to Jacob Arndt Jr. of Easton. The deed described the land as including the town of Phillipsburg.

Phillipsburg's growth was quite slow. In 1820, there were only 30 homes in Phillipsburg but, by 1847, there were 50. Phillipsburg's first growth spurt occurred in 1852, when the New Jersey Central Railroad extended its rails to Phillipsburg. By 1870, the population had soared to 5,950. On March 17, 1857, Phillipsburg Township was set off from Greenwich Township. On March 8, 1861, the state legislature approved an act that incorporated Phillipsburg as a town.

The following letter was taken from the *History of the Lehigh Valley*, by M.S. Henry, published in 1860.

"Phillipsburg may in fact be considered a part of Easton, or at least bearing the same relation to it that Camden does to Philadelphia. Many of the citizens of Easton are extensively engaged in business here, while others who are engaged in business in Easton, reside here; consequently the interests of both places are considered almost as one.

"There are two bridges over the Delaware River, which connect the town with Easton: the one a wagon-bridge, erected in 1806, and the other the celebrated double bridge of the Lehigh Valley Railroad. The old Delaware Bridge, which we crossed to reach this place, is a miracle of cleanliness, and from either side of, which, through the open windows, can be obtained a charming and romantic view. As we emerge from the bridge on the Phillipsburg side, we found ourselves within a fine large open square, which is named Union Square, and is surrounded on all sides by fine large buildings; in this square is transacted the principal mercantile business of the place. Some of the stores I noticed with the patent iron fronts and in appearance compare very favorably with the handsomest stores in Easton. Within this square are located the Post-office, Bank, Lenni Lenape, and Union Square Hotels and the depot of the Belvidere Delaware Railroad. The buildings of this depot are some of the finest and most complete in the State. The passenger building, which is about sixty feet square, is built of brick, four stories high, and was erected at a cost of about $14,000; the interior arrangement is unsurpassed for convenience. Some idea of the amount of goods received and shipped at this depot may be formed, from the size of the freight house, which is 200 feet long by 80 feet wide, and lighted through out with gas.

"The gas used in the public and private buildings is manufactured by the Easton Gas Co., and is conveyed from that place through a large iron pipe, which is laid over the Delaware Bridge.

"The town, from the fact of its not being incorporated, lacks many improvements which would greatly add to the convenience of its residents. The only accommodations for foot passengers, with but few exceptions, is a narrow plank walk, which at present is in a rather dilapidated condition. There are, however, fair prospects of the town not only becoming incorporated, but of its being made the seat of justice of a new county, which the citizens of the place and surrounding country are endeavoring to form from parts of the counties of Warren, Morris, and Hunterdon.

"In our walk through the principal avenue, we passed the handsome residence of Hon. Chas. Sitgreaves, President of the Belvidere Delaware Railroad, and one of the leading men in Western New Jersey. Immediately behind this residence is Mount Lebanon, upon which a number of the wealthier citizens have built their cottages. The view from this mountain is very fine; as it is situated directly opposite where the Lehigh empties into the Delaware, it affords a fine view up that river for the distance of about two miles, the beauty of which is greatly augmented by the smoke and flames of the furnaces and manufactories which line its banks and rise high above the lofty trees.

"From this mountain we wended our way to that of Parnassus; the view from this mountain is not so extensive as that from Lebanon, but it gives the tourist a better opportunity of seeing the many improvements in the neighborhood, of which there is probably a greater number within the circle of a thousand feet than can be found anywhere else in the Middle States.

'This beautiful mountain was named after one of the noted mountains in Greece, which it is supposed somewhat resembled this-it having two summits-one of which was consecrated to Apollo and the Muse, the other to Bacchus. On it was the celebrated Castalian fountain, the waters of which were fabled to inspire those who drank there the true spirit of poetry."

Pictured in 1905, the Bullman Street Steps lead to Bullman Street from South Main Street. There are 149 steps in all.

The Greenwich-on-the-Delaware log church stood somewhere near the present corner of Hudson and Brainerd Streets. In the back was a graveyard, which was leveled and wiped out when the Morris and Essex Railroad came to Phillipsburg in 1866. All references to the church disappeared after the Revolutionary War. The Communion cup and altar cloth (pictured above) was used in the log church. On the bottom of the cup is engraved "1761 C.A.M. I.P.B." The meaning of the initials is unknown.

One
A Religious Community

Rosa Gellock (wearing a hat) poses with her Sunday school class of St. Luke's Episcopal Church in 1915. The religious history of Phillipsburg dates to 1737, when the presbytery of New Brunswick sent a missionary to preach to the Native Americans at the Forks. In 1740, missionary David Brainerd arrived and built a log church, in which he frequently preached to both the settlers and the Native Americans. The log church stood in the valley south of the present Greenwich Church, 10 miles from the Delaware. In an interesting note about Phillipsburg's religious history, William G. Tomer, who was Phillipsburg's town health officer in 1880, composed the music to the hymn "God Be With You Till We Meet Again."

The First Presbyterian Church was organized on December 13, 1853. In 1854, Rev. Smith Sturges began construction on a church. The church was dedicated in 1888, at South Main and Market Streets. In 1961, the First Presbyterian merged with the Trinity Presbyterian Church of Delaware Park. In 1971, the old church was razed. Today, the site is a parking lot.

St. Philip and St. James Roman Catholic Church was organized in 1858. The cornerstone for the church was laid in September 1860. In 1873, construction began on a new church, which was completed in 1889. The steeple, with a clock and bell tower, was added in 1911.

The First Methodist Sunday school was formed in Phillipsburg c. 1826. Parishioners met in an old storeroom on Main Street at the southwest corner of the Central Railroad Bridge. In 1827, they moved to Easton, Pennsylvania. In 1855, the Phillipsburg group withdrew and, on May 20, 1855, the First Methodist Episcopal Church of Phillipsburg, Warren County, was organized. Services were held in the old Sitgreaves Building until August 13, 1855, when the new church was completed on South Main Street. In 1939, the First Methodist joined with the Wesley Methodist Church.

The Seventh-Day Adventist church was organized in 1934. The first service in the new church, at Hudson and Firth Streets, was held in 1950.

The Grace Evangelical Lutheran Church was organized in 1870 at Mercer and McKeen Streets. This church was razed in 1884, and a chapel was erected on South Main Street. The chapel was enlarged twice. In 1905, a large pipe organ was installed in the church. Their present church was erected on Roseberry Street in 1958.

The Phillipsburg Gospel Tabernacle of the Christian and Missionary Alliance was organized in 1926. Services were held at the North End Mission on North Main Street until the Christian and Missionary Alliance purchased the old First Methodist Church on South Main Street. In 1984, the name was changed to Emmanuel Christian Church. They disbanded in 1988–1989.

St. Luke's Episcopal Church Sunday school Class of 1911 included, from left to right, as follows: (first row) Matt Bercaw, Frank Ahart, John Exley, Elisha Lutz, and Frank White; (middle row) Johnny Lutz, Johnny Bowers, Bill Houseworth, Russ VanSyckle, and unidentified; (third row) Florence Cater (teacher), and Frank Housell.

St Luke's Free Church was formed on December 22, 1856. A Mr. Kent of the Andover Furnace Company donated land on South Main Street for the construction of the first church, which was erected in 1861 on South Main Street near the intersection of Mercer Street. In 1935, St. Paul's Chapel was erected at Morris and Warren Streets. The chapel was relocated in 1954 due to the construction of Memorial Parkway. St. Luke's Free Church and St. Paul's Chapel merged and built a new St. Luke's Episcopal Church at Hillcrest Boulevard and Lincoln Streets in 1955.

The German Evangelical Lutheran St. John's Congregation was organized on February 5, 1875, and a church was erected at Chambers and Fulton Streets in 1876. German services were discontinued c. 1910, and the name was changed to St. John's Evangelical Lutheran Church. The original church had a steeple, which was removed in 1933 after it was struck by lightning. The congregation still worships in the original church, which has undergone several renovations.

St. Peter and Paul's Slovak Church is an offshoot of St. Peter and Paul's Greek Church. It was organized on March 4, 1913, and a church was erected in 1930 on Sayre Avenue at Ann Street. In 1936, the Mass was celebrated in Latin but the sermon was given in Slovak.

On November 6, 1889, the City Mission Sunday school was organized by William E. Geil, a Lafayette College student. A permanent Baptist organization grew from this service. The first service in the South Main Street church was held on January 23, 1896. In 1911, Baptists could worship at the church on South Main Street (above) or at the Lincoln Street Chapel, Baptist Mission (below). The congregation still worships in the original church, which is now known as the Grace Baptist Church.

The Wesley Methodist Episcopal Church was organized in 1872. The church, which was erected on Lewis Street, was dedicated in January 1873. The church was consumed by fire in 1937. Immediately thereafter, a new church was erected on Miller Street. In 1939, the First Methodist Church, the Harmony Methodist Church, and the Green's Bridge Church joined with the Wesley Church to form the Wesley Methodist Church.

The Westminster Presbyterian Church was organized as a Sunday school on April 27, 1886. The congregation met in Dull's Hall until the church, on Chambers Street, was completed in 1890. Worship services are still held in the same church.

The Original Saint Peter and Paul Greek Catholic Church, which was consecrated on August 1, 1917, was located on Center Street. In 1930, a larger church was erected on South Main Street.

The North End Mission, an interdenominational mission, dates to 1868. William Wilhelm started a Sunday school for all youngsters who did not honor the Sabbath. This movement grew and, in 1887 a building was erected at North Main and Third Streets. The North End Mission ceased operations c. 1930.

Baptisms were conducted in the Delaware River at Phillipsburg's Municipal Bathing Beach, just north of the Free Bridge.

The original St John's Church was a log and straw-roofed structure erected c. 1750. This building served the local German Lutherans and Moravian Brethren for about 30 years, after which it became solely Lutheran. At that time the name was changed to St. James. In 1790, a large stone church replaced the log church. The new church had galleries around the three sides and a high pulpit. In 1834, the church was again rebuilt, this time with brick. This building still occupies the site. The church is still known as the Straw Church, although the straw roof is long gone.

Graduates of the Phillipsburg High School Class of 1886 pose for posterity.

Two
SCHOOL DAYS

Construction of the Reese School in 1890 marked Phillipsburg's third high school building. The school was named after Thomas Reese and was demolished in 1975.

The Ihrie Schoolhouse was the first erected within the present Phillipsburg limits and was located on Sitgreaves Street at the edge of a forest. The earliest teacher on record (1815) was called Old Cohen. At that time the wilderness area around the school was inhabited by snakes, which often entered the classroom. The school was named after Charles Ihrie, owner of mills in the area. It was a stone building 28 feet by 31 feet. Demolished in 1854, it became part of the Easton and Amboy Railroad bed.

From 1833 to 1838, Eliza Davis taught school in a room of a stone building on South Main Street, opposite the Bullman Street steps. This building, which in 1876 housed the *Warren Democrat*, was demolished in 1900. A second schoolroom was located in the basement of a stone building owned by the Phillipsburg Horse Car Rail Road Company at 114 North Main Street. This building was demolished in 1893. Jane Weeler was the teacher from 1838 to 1843

In 1843, the Honorable Charles Sitgreaves sold the land on South Main Street just opposite the old Elks Building, with the stipulation that a school building, no higher than one story, so as not to obstruct the view from the Sitgreaves residence, be constructed. This brick building was used as a school from 1843 to 1852. The first teacher hired was Charles Reese, who received a salary of $20 per month. The building was demolished *c.* 1875.

On October 10, 1854, land on Sitgreaves Street was purchased from George Bruch Jr. for the construction of another school. This school was known as the Furnace School. It was a two-story brick building. The first floor housed a female school, taught by H.B. Niles, who was also the principal. In 1859, a bell was installed. Before a cistern was built in 1864, water was obtained from the neighbors.

In 1860, S. Freeman opened the Lenni Lenape Institute. The exact location of this school is unknown. By 1869, there were more students than schoolrooms, so rooms were rented. One such room was located in a building on the corner of Stockton and South Main Streets. Able to accommodate up to 130 pupils, the schoolroom was in a building owned by M.M. Fisk and was known as Fisk's Hall. There was a primary and secondary department under the charge of M.M. Fisk and Kate McKinney. There was also a school building on Mercer Street. The principal's name was Fogarty, and the assistant was Mary McConnell.

In 1874, the Andover Engine House was remodeled for use as a school. The second floor housed the intermediate department, with M. Alten as teacher. The first floor was a primary school with Kate McKeeny and Lizzie Huff as teachers. This building burned down on September 13, 1875.

The Howell School was erected in 1873 at 15 Belvidere Road and was named after the area in which it was erected: Howell Flats. The teachers were J. Sheppare, principal, and Miss Burwell, assistant. The building was demolished in 1923, and a new Howell School was erected on the same site.

The Green School was named after the area in which it was erected. The first Green School, a one-room log school, was erected c. 1800. This 1911 photograph shows the second Green School. It was located on Lock Street near Ridge Street and Green's Bridge. The third and present Green School was erected in 1972 at 1000 Green Street.

St. Philip and St. James Catholic Church supported three schools. St. Philip and St. James Elementary and High School (left) was erected at South Main and Stockton Streets in 1875; Saint Catherine's Academy opened in 1887 at 518 South Main Street.

In 1961, St. Philip and St. James School was converted to an elementary school. In that year, Phillipsburg Catholic High School was erected at 137 Roseberry Street. In 1994, Phillipsburg Catholic High School closed and reopened as All Saints Elementary School.

The old Carpenter School was erected in 1864 on Sitgreaves and Abbott Streets. The construction cost was $1,914.

The William E. Harwig School was erected on Wilbur Avenue. In 1923, the school building was converted to a hospital. This was the first home of Warren Hospital. Currently, it is a nursing home.

The John Firth School was erected at Marshall and Prospect Streets in 1911.

The Bruch School was erected at 672 South Main Street in 1855. This building was named after George Bruch, who owned the land.

The Lovell Building was erected to be used as Phillipsburg's second high school and an elementary school. The building was located at the corner of Sitgreaves and South Main Streets. The school was named after Jacob R. Lovell, an early superintendent of schools. After the Lovell School closed, the Lovell Building became the home of the Phillipsburg Municipal Building (1913–1971). The Lovell Building was demolished in 1975. The present Phillipsburg Municipal Building is located on Corliss Avenue.

The Lovell School was photographed in 1900.

The Freeman School was erected on Filmore Street in 1869. The school was named after Samuel Freeman. Built at a cost of $46,131.84, the school was nicknamed the Crystal Palace because of its elaborate interior. This building was demolished in 1940, and a new Freeman School was erected on the same site.

The Reese School (right), was Phillipsburg's third high school building. The Lovell School (left) became the Phillipsburg Municipal Building in 1913, two years after this photograph was taken. Both buildings were demolished in 1975.

The Barber School was erected at 574 Sargent Avenue in 1931.

A group of unidentified children pose in front of the Barber School in the late 1930s.

The first Sitgreaves School was erected in 1851 at 53 Brainerd Street. This building was demolished in 1893. A new Sitgreaves School was built on the same site. The school, named after Phillipsburg's first mayor, Charles Sitgreaves, was nicknamed the Old Academy. This building was demolished in 1975.

The Brensinger School was erected at Congress and Mill Streets. The school was named after Joseph H. Brensinger. This building has been demolished.

The present Phillipsburg High School was erected in 1928 on Hillcrest Boulevard. This picture was taken shortly after its completion.

The Saints Peter and Paul Parochial School was opened on September 5, 1922. The Sisters of the Third Order of St. Francis were placed in charge.

All Saints Regional Catholic School was erected as Phillipsburg Catholic High School at 137 Roseberry Street in 1961. The high school closed in 1994 and reopened as an elementary school. This is a celebration of the first open-air Mass in Phillipsburg, on August 29, 1971.

Members of this c. 1912 class at St. Philip and St. James School are, from left to right, as follows: (first row) two unidentified students, J. Sweeney, B. Tighe, R. O'Brian, S. McIntosh, and F. Ashman; (second row) M. Connor Boyle, "Sis" Monahan, M. Conlain, M. Smith, C. Smith, unidentified, M. Ashman, A. McClafferty Wyant, and M. Hickey; (third row) K. Kupcha, C. Smith, H. Lynch, M. Kane, unidentified, F. Bach, and R. Dicker; (fourth row) M. McHugh, M. McCann, M. Lansey, unidentified, M Cipp, A. Shields, and M. Stacer; (fifth row) all unidentified.

The Pursell Hill School students pose in front of the Pursell Hill School in 1898.

The L.O. Beers School was erected in 1919 at 582 South Main Street.

A decorated Standard Silk Mill wagon is in front of the mill in 1911. Phillipsburg celebrated its 50th year on March 8, 1911.

Three
INDUSTRY

The interior of the Phillipsburg Steam Bakery, located at South Main and Stockton Streets, is shown c. 1910. This is the present site of the Lock Doctor. This bakery was owned and operated by Jacob Ottenbacher, seen at the extreme right.

The town of Phillipsburg was a good location for manufacturing enterprises. Phillipsburg was only two hours by rail from New York and Philadelphia. It was also close to the anthracite coal mines and pig iron furnaces in Pennsylvania. With the onset of the Industrial Revolution, Phillipsburg boomed. In 1860, the population of Phillipsburg was only 1,500. By 1870, the population grew by 300 percent to 5,950.

The first company to locate in Phillipsburg was J.R. Templin's Iron and Brass Foundry, which had been established in 1848. This company supplied the iron pillars for the Crystal Palace in New York City. Unfortunately, the foundry was consumed by fire on July 4, 1855, and was never rebuilt.

Around the same time, in 1848, the first furnace of the Cooper Iron Works was built. Brothers Peter and Edward Cooper and A. S. Hewitt founded this company which, in 1867, became the Andover Iron Company. The company was located along South Main Street just past the present Andover-Morris Elementary School building. By 1900, the Andover Iron Company was turning out 50,000 tons of pig iron annually.

The third company to move to Phillipsburg was Reese & Company, which began in 1849 and which manufactured agricultural implements. The financial panic of 1873 is blamed for driving this company out of business. It closed its doors in 1876.

The oldest industry currently in Phillipsburg is the Warren Foundry & Machine Company. This company was chartered in 1856. It erected a plant on Sitgreaves Street between Stockton and McKeen Streets. In 1894, it expanded and covered property from Center to Stockton Streets. The company is currently known as Atlantic States Cast Iron Pipe Company.

The J.T. Baker Company opened in Phillipsburg in 1904. In 1941, it became a division of the Vick Chemical Company, which is currently known as Mallinckrodt Baker Chemical Company.

During the 1960s, Ingersoll-Rand was Phillipsburg's largest employer. This company opened in Phillipsburg in 1903 after repeated floods along the Lehigh River disrupted its West Easton, Pennsylvania plant. In 1911, a separate plant was built to house the A.S. Cameron Pump Works, which was acquired in 1909. Most of Ingersoll-Rand has been relocated out of Phillipsburg.

The first inhabitants of Phillipsburg mostly were German. The industrial growth brought new nationalities. The Irish were the first to appear. The first Irish were immigrant laborers on the railroads. They brought to the area new names, such as Kenney, O'Brien, O'Hara, and McCann. The area from Sitgreaves to Howard Streets was the area in which most of the Irish immigrants settled. Later, this area was inhabited largely by Italian immigrants.

Right: The largest pipe ever made at the Warren Foundry & Machine Company was photographed *c.* 1925. In the center in bib overalls is C. Exley. Behind him, with an arm raised, is J. Tirrell. To the left of Exley, in a tie and vest, is plant superintendent L. Exley.

The Warren Foundry & Machine Company was located on Sitgreaves Street. This is a 1905 view of the plant.

Employees of the Canister Company of New Jersey pose in 1922. This company manufactured the Canwood canister, which was sold throughout the world. Located on North Broad Street, the company began operations in 1899.

In 1955, Sunoco Products of Garwood opened a branch in the old Canister Company building, on Broad Street. Sunoco Products manufactured tubing cores and spools of paper and fiber for the construction industry.

D.D. Juillard & Company founded the Standard Silk Mill on May 3, 1886. In 1911, the company employed 1,500 people. The company erected a building, which housed a YWCA and tennis courts for its female employees and a baseball field for its male employees.

Employees of the Standard Silk Mill pause from their work for this photograph c. 1898. Third from the right in the front row is Helen Nora Duckworth, who later married William Eldridge.

The Cooper-Andover Furnace Company, on South Main Street across from Limekiln Road, is shown c. 1890. This site is currently occupied by a gas station and the Andover-Morris Elementary School.

In September 1869, Jacob Tippett, an employee of Selders & Kent, purchased Selders's interest in the company. As a result the company, which manufactured water tanks and standpipes, was renamed Tippett and Kent. In 1871, Kent sold his interest to Tippett. In 1873, J.W. Wood purchased an interest in the company, which was then renamed Tippett & Wood. The company was located on Howard Street.

The original administration building of the J.T. Baker Chemical Company, on North Broad Street, is shown in the early 1920s. J.T. Baker began operations in Phillipsburg in 1904. The company continued to expand and, in 1956, opened a modern research facility. The company is currently known as the Mallinckrodt Baker Chemical Company.

Baker Chemical employees of 1910 are, from left to right, as follows: (front row) J. Dick, B. Rush, S. Mickel, unidentified, C. Thatcher, C. Seibold, and R. Frey; (middle row) T. Bryan, K. Sceartz, and W. Hartman; (back row) M. Mickel, E. Weidman, W. Lutz, and unidentified.

The Vulcan Iron Works began operations in March 1871. J. Protz, F.F. Drinkhouse, and C. Weaver started this company, which manufactured harness snaps made of malleable iron. Drinkhouse became the sole proprietor and changed the name to American Horse Shoe Company. The company manufactured horseshoes, mule shoes, and toe calks. It was located in what was then known as Rolling Mills Flats. Today, the Delaware Toll Bridge crosses the Delaware River at this point. Drinkhouse family members still live in this area.

Employees of the American Horse Shoe Company take part in the November 11, 1918 Armistice Day Parade on Broad Street. Of the three men in the front, D.A. Wismer is the one on the left.

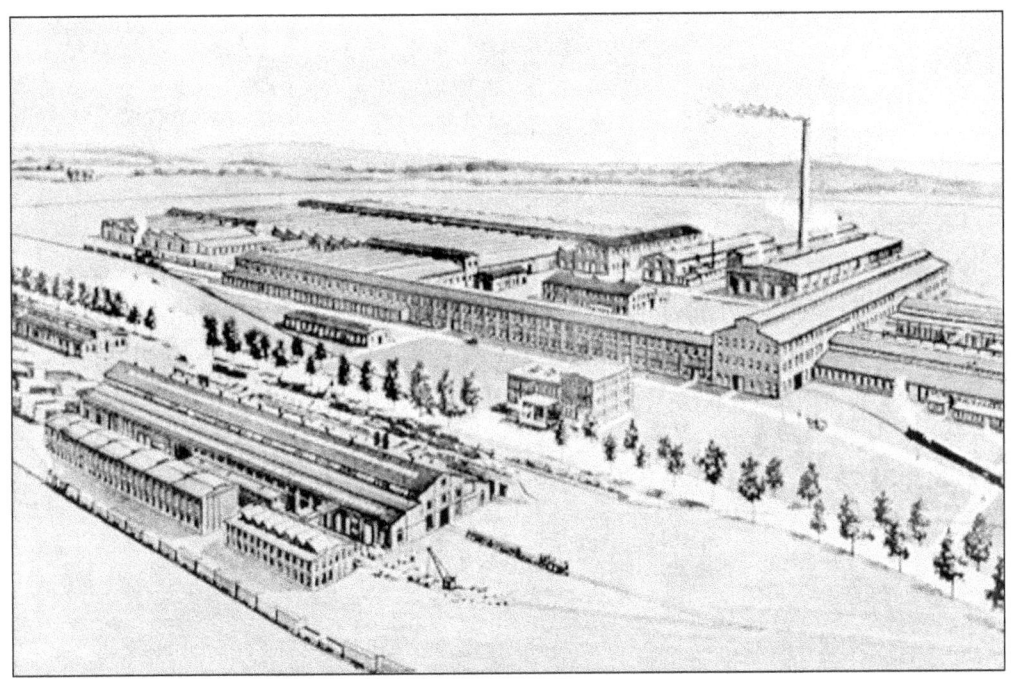

At one time there were more than 110 buildings and 10 miles of railroad tracks on the 200 acres of land occupied by the Ingersoll-Rand Company. The company manufactured pumps, drills, and jackhammers of all types. Many of these items can be found on ocean oil-drilling rigs.

The Ingersoll-Rand Employees' Band poses on July 1, 1916, in front of the Ravenswood Building near Fairmount Cemetery. The young man in the center leaning on the bass drum is 12-year-old Charlie Knecht.

The Rowland Firth & Son Company, located in the Rolling-Mill Flats along Broad Street, manufactured grinding mills. In 1911, it was one of the main manufacturers of steel castings for the many cement mills in the area.

I.S. Snyder's Carriage Works was located at the rear of present 400 block of South Main Street. This photograph was taken c. 1880.

Employees of the Tippett & Wood Company take a break from work. The c. 1920 photograph was taken inside the Howard Street plant. Phillipsburg had many other industries. J.O. Wagner, J. Evans, and A. Wilhelm started the American Sheet Iron Company in 1869. The Delaware Rolling Mill, started by J. Semple, was commonly known as the Forge. Instead of being rolled, the iron was forged into bars with a trip-hammer. When the company moved from Easton, Pennsylvania, to Phillipsburg, it abandoned the trip-hammer method and used rolls. The American Brick & Tile Company, established in 1886, made bricks from pulverized slate. Bricks made of this material are far superior to bricks made of clay. In 1890, the American Brick & Tile Company produced 20,000 bricks per day. Its bricks were used in streets and pavements throughout the area. The Phillipsburg Water Works was built in 1886. The distributing mains, which extended for 12 miles, were manufactured by the Warren Foundry in Phillipsburg. The L.C. Smith Bobbin Works of Phillipsburg, founded in 1917, specialized in bobbins for the silk industry and spools for the cotton trade. Tirrell Brothers, Phillipsburg Silk Company, Wallace Silk Corporation, Tilton Silk Company, Warren Throwing Company, and the Standard Silk Mill were located in Phillipsburg.

Walter Cutsler, pictured c. 1913, joined the Phillipsburg police force on February 17, 1913. He patrolled the seventh ward (note the 7 on his hat). On May 26, 1926, he became police chief, and he served in this capacity until his death at age 71 in 1938.

Four
PUBLIC SERVICE

The Jersey Hose Fire Company No. 2 runners and racing cart were in use from 1881 to 1915.

The first fire company organized in Phillipsburg was the Warren Fire Company, on August 8, 1864. The group's motto was "We strive for the good of all." The company was disbanded in the late 1870s due to lack of support. The second company was the Andover Engine Company, which organized in 1867. Their engine house was located on South Main Street. In 1873, the old engine house was converted into a schoolhouse. On the morning of September 13, 1875, the building was consumed by fire.

The Jersey Hose Company No. 2 was organized on April 15, 1887. The company's motto was "Duty is our pride." The group erected an engine house on the site of the old Andover Engine House, on South Main Street. The first fire fought by the Jersey Hose Company was at the home of John Ruef, at 507 South Main Street. The Centennial Engine Company was organized on January 27, 1875. This unit was praised for its action at the Pardee Hall fire at Lafayette College in 1897. The group disbanded on April 28, 1914, reorganized on May 19, 1914, as the Phillipsburg Fire Company No. 1, and set up quarters on Market Street. This company purchased the first motorized fire apparatus to be placed in service in Phillipsburg. The motorized apparatus was an Oldsmobile Touring Car converted to carry a tank and hose box. After the engine house was destroyed by fire, a new house was erected at 220 South Main Street.

The Reliance Hose Company No. 1 was organized on February 8, 1887. Its house was located at 292 Chambers Street. This is Phillipsburg's oldest firefighting organization still operating. Currently, it is located at Firth and Marshall Streets. The Alert Hook & Ladder Company was organized on May 31, 1887. It was located at 209 Chambers Street until moving to Firth and Marshall Streets in 1989. The Warren Chemical Fire Company was founded on January 25, 1908. Today, it is located on Pursell's Hill. The Lincoln Engine Company No. 2 was organized on February 12, 1909, on Lincoln Street. Its first hand-pulled fire engine came from the defunct Centennial Engine Company. The company moved into its present house at 354 Lincoln Street on July 14, 1939. The Huntington Volunteer Fire Company No. 1 was organized in January 1946. In 1969, the company constructed a new station. The Delaware Park Chemical Engine Company No. 1 was incorporated on January 12, 1911. It erected a firehouse at 112 Park Avenue.

With the words "And be it enacted that the Common Council of said town shall have the power to appoint a high constable and such assistance as they may judge proper to hold there respectively during the pleasure of the Common Council and to proscribe there duties power and compensation . . . ," which were written in Section 10 of the original Town Charter of Phillipsburg on March 8, 1861, a police department was established. The duties of the constables were to prevent the running at large of cattle, horses, sheep, goats, swine, and geese, and to suppress disorderly gambling houses and "groggeries."

Gen. William Maxwell and Martha Washington passed through Phillipsburg on June 16, 1779. Mrs. Washington was on her way to Mount Vernon, and Maxwell was her escort. In October 1779, Gen. John Sullivan's expedition encamped in and around Phillipsburg. On July 26, 1782, Gen. George Washington came to Phillipsburg on his way to set up camp in Newburgh, New York.

Phillipsburg has many notable military people among its former inhabitants. Gen. Joseph Warren was a hero of the American Revolution who lost his life in the Battle of Bunker Hill on June 17, 1775. Sgt. Richard Holmes raised the Colorado regimental colors on the heights of Malate at Manilain in the Spanish-American War and earned the nickname "Bullet-Proof Dick, the hero of Malate." George F. Mager, a seaman during the Spanish-American War, was awarded the Medal of Honor. Pvt. 1st Class Martin O. May was posthumously awarded the Medal of Honor for his heroic deeds on Ie Shima during World War II. Charles Heckman was a sergeant in the Mexican-American War. During the Civil War he enlisted in the Union Army as a major and later earned promotions to colonel and brevet major general. He was captured at the Battle of Drury's Bluff in 1864 but was released in exchange for several Confederate prisoners.

The Jersey Hose Company No. 2 was organized on April 15, 1887. Members stand in front of their firehouse on South Main Street c. 1900. In 1957, the company moved to its new house at 540 South Main Street.

Alert Hook & Ladder Company No. 1 was organized on May 31, 1887. Its house was at 209 Chambers Street. Among the members pictured in this 1929 photograph are driver L. Silverthorn; Chief E. Kocher, in the black uniform; G. Stewart and ? Dilts, both sitting on the running board; and Shorty Butler, standing to the right of Dilts.

The Phillipsburg Fire Company No. 1 was organized on May 19, 1914, replacing the former Centennial Engine Company No. 1. The company were located on Market Street until its house was destroyed by fire. The company erected a new house at 220 South Main Street.

The Delaware Park Chemical Engine Company No. 1 was organized on September 13, 1910. The firehouse is at 112 Park Avenue. Shown are, from left to right, C. Miller, J. Miers, T. Thacher, E. Rodenbough, and W. Hackman. The utility car was converted into the company's first ambulance in 1948.

The Lincoln Fire Company No. 2 was organized on February 12, 1909. This photograph was taken on Lincoln Street near Marshall Street in 1911. On July 14, 1939, the company moved into its new house at 354 Lincoln Street.

The Reliance Hose Company No.1 was organized on February 8, 1887. The firehouse was located at 292 Chambers Street. Today, it is located at Firth and Marshall Streets.

The Centennial Engine Company was organized on January 26, 1876. On May 19, 1914, it became the Phillipsburg Fire Company No. 1. This picture was taken in 1911 in front of the group's Market Street firehouse.

The Warren Chemical Fire Company was organized on January 25, 1908. The firehouse was on Mill Street. The company is now located on Columbus Street.

The Phillipsburg Police Department is shown outside city hall, 160 South Main Street, in this photograph taken c. 1911.

For many years, the Centennial Engine Company No. 1 station was also police headquarters. Standing in back of William Fisher, police commissioner, in this 1926 photograph are, from left to right, "Dory" Booth, T. "Slim" Kane, L. "Lew" Silverthorn, D. "Dan" Hogan, L. "Hoffy" Hoff, T. Halley, R. Brotzman, C. Segreaves, J. "Honus" Kauffman, J. "Jake" Taylor, Chief W. Cutsler, K. "Red" Vandegrift (killed in the line of duty in 1930), C. "Bud" Graham, and A. "Sparky" Hedden.

Members of the 1904 Phillipsburg Police Department posing at the Centennial Firehouse are, from left to right, as follows: (front row) Chief Gorgas; F. Kneedler, town clerk; J. Firth, mayor; and T. Wilson; (second row) D. Snyder, J. Taylor, S. Stokes, D. Hogan, C. Hans, and T. "Slim" Kane.

The Keystone Kops and Kangaroo Kort were part of Phillipsburg's centennial celebrations in 1961. Shown, from left to right, are D. Rounsaville, W. Jones, magistrate J. Brennan, E. Deacon III, W. Bartholomew Sr., "Clancy" Rounsaville, and D. Jiorle.

In nearby Alpha, the police were on horseback in 1928. In the left distance is St. John's Russian Orthodox Greek Catholic Church, located on Second Avenue.

Some of the young men from Phillipsburg drafted into the armed services in 1941 are, from left to right, as follows: (front row) V. Belardinelli, G.S. Elmo, T. Frinzi, L.P. Pretopapa, and E. Firman; (middle row) W. Lansche, F.J. Frye, F.B. Knecht, and W.A. Struther: (back row) W.T. Hess, E.J. Fauerbach, W.R. Howell, D.K. Campbell, and S. Palinkas Jr.

Veterans of the Spanish-American War and the Civil War march in the Civil War Memorial Dedication Parade, which was held on May 10, 1906.

Members of the Phillipsburg Home Guard pose at Ortygia Hall on Hanover Street on February 27, 1918. Behind M. Stocker (seated in front) are, from left to right, the following: (front row) F. Randall, G. Lodge, R. Kirkendall, C. Schnoor, W. Person, H. Jones, H. Henshaw, C. Jago, and C. Pursell; (middle row) J. Salzeman, H. Snyder, H. Rush, H. Reinhardt, R. Burge, W. Henry, and R. Lambert; (third row) H. Troxell, C. Rush, J. Henshaw, Lt. M. Guthrie Jr., C. Weiss, W. Peacher, and W. Kussler.

The World War II bomber *City of Phillipsburg, New Jersey* was paid for by the citizens of Phillipsburg. For this photograph, the name was placed on the side of the plane. Afterward, the name was taken down and that of another community was placed on the plane.

Maj. Gen. Charles A. Heckman, above, one of many war heroes from Phillipsburg, enlisted as a sergeant in the Mexican-American War. After the war he was a conductor for the Central Railroad of New Jersey. He later enlisted in the Union Army and was a major in the 9th Regiment of New Jersey Volunteers. He was promoted to colonel and major general. He was captured at the Battle of Drury's Bluff on May 16, 1864. After several months he was exchanged for several Confederate prisoners. He then took command of the 18th Army Corps. His troops captured Fort Harrison and 2,000 prisoners. In 1865, he was given command of the 25th Army Corps. He resigned from service in 1865.

Gen. Joseph Warren was a hero of the American Revolution who lost his life in the Battle of Bunker Hill on June 17, 1775. Warren County was named after him.

The Mutchler family of Phillipsburg had more sons in the Civil War than any other family in America. Six brothers enlisted in the Union Army, and one brother enlisted in the Confederate Army. They all earned commissions. The only fatality was Sgt. William Mutchler, who was killed while leading his unit, Company E 7th Regiment, at Williamsburg, Virginia, on May 5, 1862.

Sgt. Richard G. Holmes was born in Phillipsburg on January 24, 1875. A graduate of Phillipsburg High School and Lafayette College, he was a star football player who went on to play for a Denver football team. While in Denver he signed with the Colorado Volunteers during the Spanish-American War. He was in charge of Company 1, the color companies. He planted the Colorado regiment colors on the heights of Malate at Manila and was thereafter known as "Bullet-Proof Dick, the hero of Malate." He is shown with Gov. Thompson of Colorado.

Pvt. 1st Class Martin O. May was posthumously awarded the Medal of Honor, America's highest military service award, for extreme heroic circumstances. During World War II, May gallantly maintained a three-day stand on the slopes of Iegusubuyama on Ie Shima, Ryukyu Island. On April 19, 1945, he broke up an attack and counterattacked from his machine-gun post. He volunteered to stay and cover the movement of American soldiers as they reorganized. He was wounded and his machine gun was rendered useless by a mortar shell. He then began throwing hand grenades until he was mortally wounded.

Robert B. Meyner was born on July 3, 1908, in Easton, Pennsylvania. He graduated from Phillipsburg High School in 1926, Lafayette College in 1930, and Columbia University in 1933. He was head of the Phillipsburg Chamber of Commerce, a New Jersey state senator, and a two-term governor of New Jersey (1956–1962). While governor, he married Helen Day Stevenson, a niece of Adlai Stevenson. Meyner passed away on May 22, 1990. he is the only one of the state's chief executives to come from Warren County.

Maj. Charles Sitgreaves was born in Phillipsburg on April 22, 1803. On March 8, 1861, he was elected the first mayor of Phillipsburg. He received his A.M. degree from Princeton University in 1852 and was a practicing lawyer. In 1846, he was the public school superintendent and, from 1843 to 1854, a trustee of Lafayette College. He was the first president of the Phillipsburg National Bank, the first president of the Belvidere Delaware Railroad, a New Jersey state senator from 1852 to 1854, and a member of Congress from 1865 to 1869.

William Jennings Bryan stopped in town during a campaign speech. He is shown on Mercer Street on October 23, 1908.

Pres. Theodore Roosevelt also visited during the 1904 campaign. He gave a speech from a railroad car at the Lehigh Valley Railroad Station in Phillipsburg in October 1904.

Dr. Thomas Barber (1915) was a physician in Phillipsburg and a state senator. His brother Dr. Isaac Barber was founder of Warren Hospital. Barber Elementary School is named after Isaac Barber.

Five
MEDICAL CARE

An Ingersoll-Rand ambulance is shown c. 1900. The first physician in the Phillipsburg area was Dr. John Cooper. Cooper came to Phillipsburg in 1791 from Long Hills in Morris County. Cooper lived at the home of Capt. Henry Bidleman in the area then known as Bidleman's, now known as Green's Bridge. After four years, Cooper moved to Easton, Pennsylvania. For the following 50 years, the citizens of Phillipsburg had to travel to Easton or Greenwich Township for their medical needs. Many of the locals went to holistic healers Jacob Reese and his son Heram Reese. In 1843, Dr. Henry Southand moved to Phillipsburg but stayed only two years. In 1850, Dr. T. Stewart came to Phillipsburg, but after a short stay he moved to Scranton, Pennsylvania. Once the railroad came, so did more physicians.

Other physicians to practice in Phillipsburg were Dr. Asher Reiley (1854), Dr. J.F. Sheppard (1854), Dr. K. Espy (1855–1857), Dr. Dayton (1857), Dr. Hart (1857–1859), Dr. Osmund (1865), Dr. D.R. DeLong (1867–1869), Dr. O'Brien (1867–1871), Dr. A.H. Lee (1868), Dr. P. H. Purcell (1864), Dr. F.P. Sheppard (1866), Dr. D.X.J. Brittain (1868), Dr. H.H. Abernathy (1867–1869, 1875–1877), Dr. E.H. Beeber (1869), and Dr. J.H. Griffith (1870), who had a large practice and walked to visit his patients.

By 1897, the physicians stayed around for longer periods. Dr. Isaac Barber began his practice in Phillipsburg in 1879 and became active in political affairs. Barber was the first chief of staff of Warren Hospital. Dr. J.M. Reese (1883), in addition to caring for a large practice, found time to become involved in civic affairs. Dr. A.P. Jacoby (1888) was both a druggist and physician. Dr. F.J. Drake (1902) was the first school physician. Dr. William Kline (1891) was involved in the founding of Warren Hospital. Dr. Thomas Barber, like his brother Isaac Barber, was involved in political affairs and served as a state senator and chief of medical staff at Warren Hospital. Dr. Alma Williston was Phillipsburg's first female physician. She served as health officer and town physician. Dr. Frank Wolf (1911) was the first surgeon in chief of Warren Hospital. Dr. Paul Drake (1926) was the first resident physician at Warren Hospital.

Dr. Isaac Barber saw the need to care for indigent individuals who were denied charitable benefits out of state. Mary Lesher Reese and Isaac Barber began Warren Hospital. Reese donated $7,000 to the hospital, a considerable amount in 1923 standards. The old William F. Harwig School building on Wilbur Avenue was purchased for $1,500 and was converted into a hospital. In 1923, the Maternity Hospital and Infantorium of Warren County opened. There were 60 beds. Sometime later, the name was shortened to Warren Hospital. In 1925, a nurses training school opened. The school was short lived, closing in 1933.

In 1937, plans were laid out to build a new hospital. Not enough money was raised so, in 1941, the plan was revised and an addition was constructed. In 1954, plans again were laid out to build a new hospital, this time to be built on an eight-and-a-half-acre site on Roseberry Street donated by Ingersoll-Rand. The new hospital opened in December 1958. The first baby to be born at the hospital was Gary Warren Velekei, at 9:19 a.m. on December 13, 1958.

On May 17, 1936, the Phillipsburg Emergency Squad was formed. The squad's first call was to assist a man who had fallen from a pole. On October 25, 1949, the Delaware Park Chemical Engine Company No. 1 firehouse was designated as a highway first aid station. Later the station became the home of the Lopatcong Emergency Squad.

Warren Hospital, on Wilbur Avenue, is shown in 1929. Today, it is a nursing home.

Shown are, from left to right, Mrs. William Higginson, Minnie Verrilli, Mrs. John Geiger, Ellen Peterson, Virginia Burzycki, Marjorie Hubbard, Mrs. William Brandow, Mrs. Hans Smith, Mrs. Allen Mayberry, and Mrs. Gilver Riddle at the 25th anniversary of the Nearly New Shop in 1969.

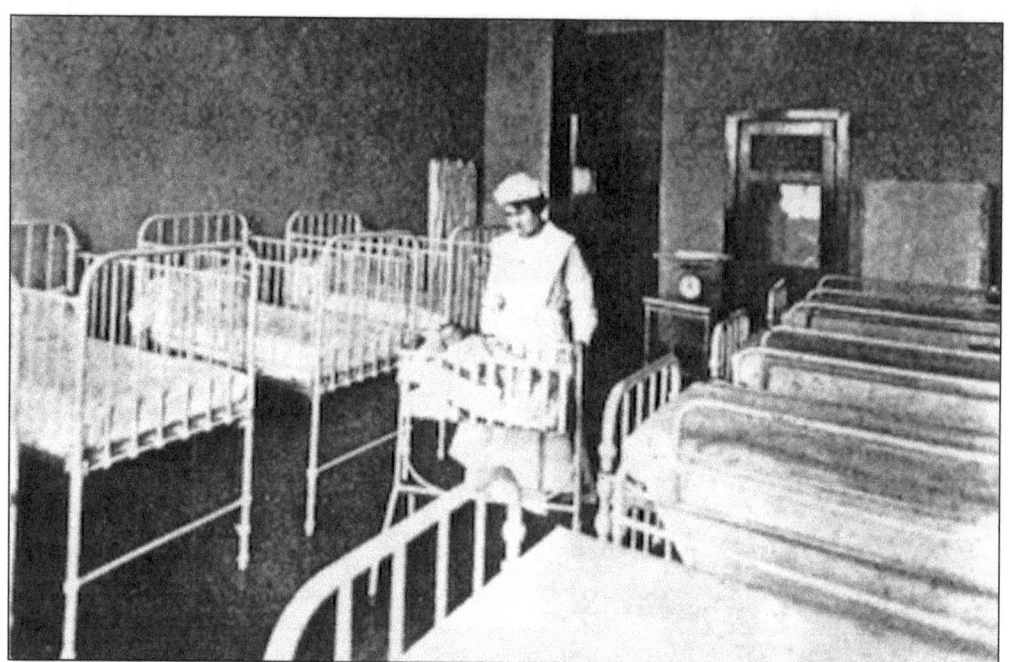

This 1929 photograph shows the children's ward at the old Warren Hospital, on Wilbur Street.

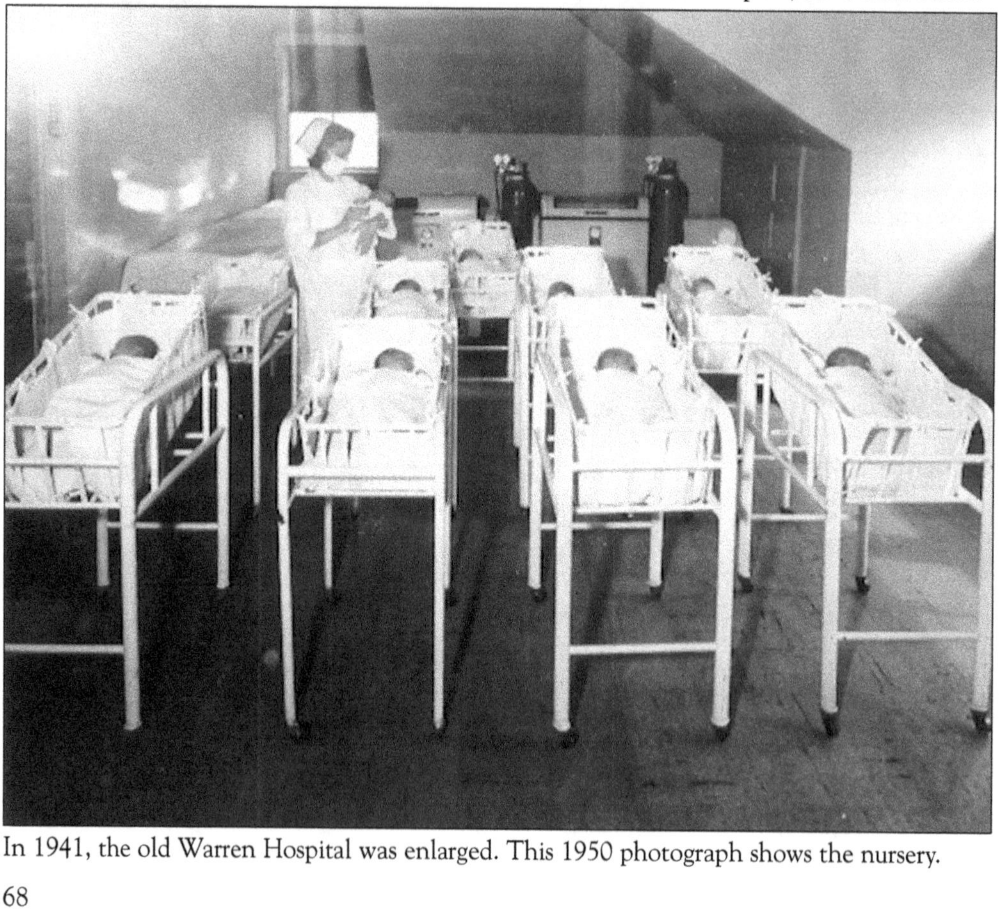

In 1941, the old Warren Hospital was enlarged. This 1950 photograph shows the nursery.

This is the solarium at the old Warren Hospital, on Wilbur Street, as it appeared in 1929.

This is the lobby of the new Warren Hospital, on Roseberry Street, as it appeared in 1980.

The new Warren Hospital opened on Roseberry Street in December 1958. This photograph was taken shortly afterward.

This is how the new Warren Hospital, on Roseberry Street, appeared in 1995 after several expansion projects, accomplished over the years.

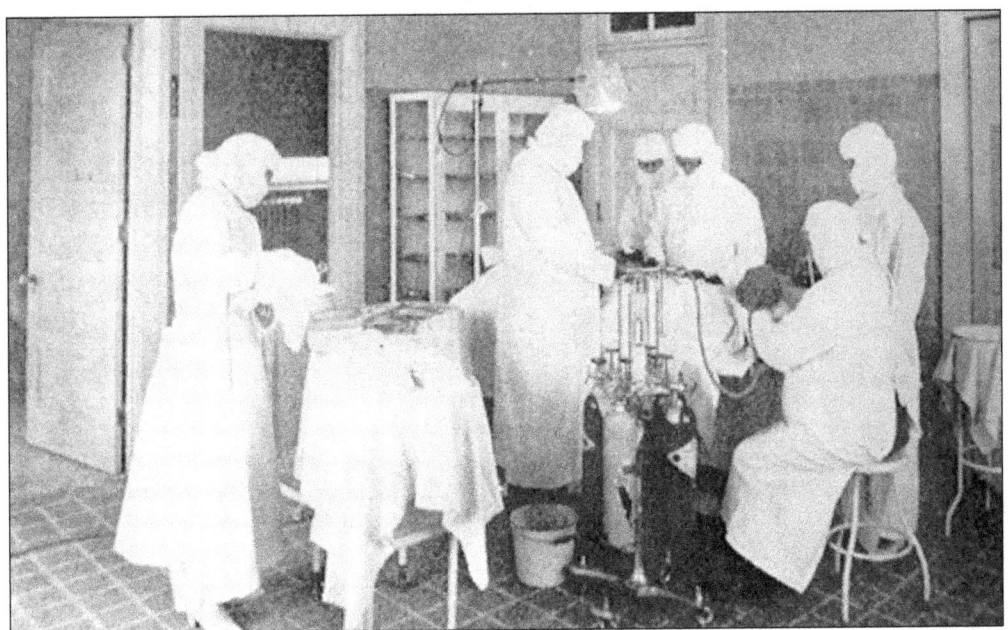
This is the operating room of the old Warren Hospital as it appeared in 1929.

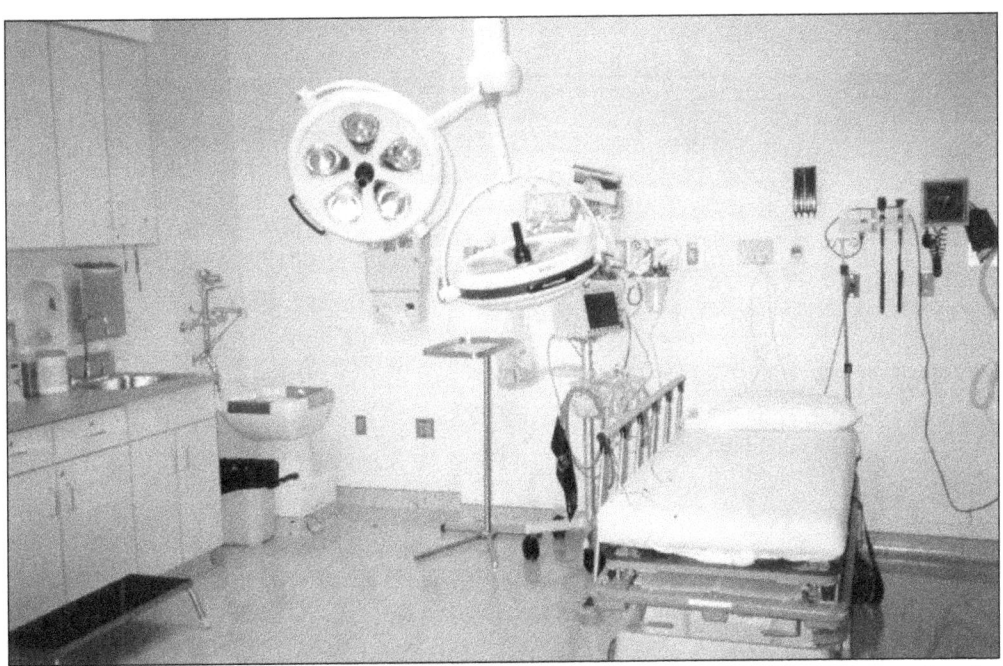
This is the emergency trauma room at the new Warren Hospital, on Roseberry Street, after the most recent expansion, which took place in 2001.

The Delaware Park Fire Company ambulance and crew in the 1950s includes, from left to right, the following: (front row) A. Bouton, J. Miers, C. Clymer, E. Clymer, K. Mellert, C. Cymer, H. Streepy, W. Stires Jr., and E. Rodenbough; (back row) C. Miller, C. Fulmer, H. Deremer, and H. Lawrence.

A 1947 International truck, belonging to the Phillipsburg Emergency Squad, was housed at the Lincoln Firehouse. This was said to be a hospital on wheels.

Members of the Phillipsburg Chapter of the National Red Cross Hostesses pose in the Red Cross Building at the New York World's Fair in 1939. They are, from left to right, Mrs. Fred Drake, Neva Harmon, Rena Bottinelli, and Ruth Reiter.

Baumgartner's Tailor and Dry Cleaning Shop was at 478 South Main Street. Shown near the shop's doorway in 1918 is the Baumgartner family, from left to right, Joseph Baumgartner, Frances Baumgartner (Wellen), Mary Baumgartner holding William Baumgartner, and young Mary Baumgartner (Perry).

Six
LOCAL MERCHANTS

The interior of Stem & Smith's, at 411 South Main Street, looked like this in 1909. Stem & Smith's was a wholesale liquor dealer.

Photographed at Stone's Department Store, at 401 South Main Street, on December 22, 1973, are, from left to right, Florence Stone, Samuel Stone, and Muretta Weisel. This picture was taken on the store's last day of business. Samuel Stone passed away on March 15, 2001.

Local merchants are the backbone of every town. Phillipsburg was no exception. Here, there was a merchant almost on every corner. There were markets, restaurants, hotels, saloons, and many other gathering places. The 1923, the West Directory lists 6 auto dealers, 4 auto supply dealers, 2 auto repairers, 1 upholsterer, 7 bakers, 3 banks, 17 barbers, 2 blacksmiths, 2 book stores, 2 shoe stores, 13 butchers, 4 chiropractors, 9 cigar and tobacco stores, 2 clothing stores, 7 coal yards, 4 dentists, 33 dressmakers, 6 drugstores, 6 dry goods stores, 6 electricians, 3 fish stores, 2 florists, 2 flour-and-feed mills, 2 fruit dealers, 5 furniture stores, 83 grocery stores, 1 hairdresser, 2 hardware stores, 21 hotels, 2 ice dealers, 18 insurance dealers, 1 jeweler, 3 junk dealers, 1 locksmith, 5 milk dealers, 1 record store, 3 photographers, 2 printers, 12 restaurants and cafes, 15 shoemakers, 8 tailors, 2 taxi services, 2 theaters, 4 tinsmiths, 3 undertakers, 1 variety store, and many other entrepreneurs.

This 1906 view shows M. Joseph Cannon's Coal & Wood yard, at 206–208 Mercer Street. In 1905, M. Joseph Cannon purchased the business, which had been established in 1877.

In 1906, the firms of Smith & Gavin and the Murphy Brothers joined to form the Phillipsburg Supply & Construction Company. The main offices were at 43 Sitgreaves Street, and the Scranton coal yard, the largest such plant in the country, was located on Stockton Street in Phillipsburg.

The interior of Alpaugh & Sampson Grocery and Dry Goods Store, on South Main Street, is shown in 1908. A.R. Alpaugh established the business in 1886.

The interior of A.R. Alpaugh's Wallpaper Store, at 499 South Main Street, is shown in 1907. A.R. Alpaugh and a Mr. Willever established the business. Upon the retirement of Willever in 1906, Alpaugh assumed control.

Residents of Phillipsburg enjoy pizza at their favorite pizza spot, Chico's, located at 296 South Main Street. Shown in this 1963 photograph, from left to right, are Marian Manasseri, Sandy Soffera, Mary ?, unidentified, John Ballard, unidentified, owner Frank "Chico" Manasseri, and Sam Indorato.

Adam Martin is behind the counter in this 1910 photograph of his grocery store, located on the northeast corner of Stockton and South Main Streets.

C.E. Griffin established a drugstore in 1892. The interior of his store, at 29 South Main Street, is shown as it appeared in 1909.

The R.C. Bowers Wallpaper Store, at 21 Union Square, was established in 1870 as Carhart & Son, at 27 South Main. The business dealt in wallpaper, room moldings, and window shades. The photograph dates from 1909.

The Madison Square Hotel, at 299 Filmore Street, boasted 13 sleeping rooms and accommodated up to 50 people in the dining room. The photograph dates from 1909.

Louis Winkler (right) ran the largest and most successful wholesale and retail tobacco and cigar establishment in the area. His store was located at 11 Union Square The business was established in 1879, and Winkler took it over in 1881. In an advertisement in the 1909 *Free Press*, Phillipsburg recognizes Winkler's as "one of our most important business houses" and congratulates itself "on this establishment."

James Makris began selling hot dogs in Center Square in Easton, Pennsylvania, in 1908. In 1910, he moved to Phillipsburg and opened Jim's Doggie Stand in Union Square. His first stand was located to the left of the bridge entrance. Sometime in the late 1940s, he moved to the right side of the bridge and erected a new stand called the Original Frankfurter. The building was destroyed in 1966 by a pickup truck. Jimmy's Hot Dogs then reopened in a nearby store. Today, it is located in the 25th Street Shopping Center in Palmer Township, Pennsylvania.

Hoffman's Ice Cream Store was located at 375 South Main Street. It is shown here in 1913.

This 1961 photograph shows Jim's second Doggie Stand, located in Union Square just northeast of the Northampton Street Bridge.

Huff's Liquor Store was founded in 1939. Located on Memorial Parkway, the store is pictured in 1961.

The Family Liquor & Wine Store, at Sitgreaves and Stockton Streets, is shown in 1961. Mr. and Mrs. Nelson Becci purchased the store from Mr. and Mrs. Ciro Ghetti in 1949, when it was located at 98 Sitgreaves Street.

Shown in this 1900 photograph outside J.F. Butz's Barbershop in Union Square are, from left to right, Earl Butz, J.F. Butz, and unidentified.

Revere W. Hagerty's Ice Wagon was located at the corner of South Main and Hudson Streets. This photograph dates from 1915.

The Phillipsburg Daily Press building was located below Union Square on North Main Street. This picture was taken in 1912.

Eddie Moy's Steak House was a well-known spot. The owner, Eddie Moy, stands behind the counter (below). He was a professional boxer who, in 1921, unsuccessfully fought for the Lightweight Championship of the World. In 1914, he fought a draw in the last 20-round match in California. He had a boxing ring in the basement of his steak house, which he encouraged kids to use as an alternative to getting into street fights.

For Phillipsburg's Diamond Jubilee, in 1936, many recreational activities were planned. This one was the Easter Egg Hunt for children.

Seven
RECREATION AND SPORTS

The Municipal Bathing Beach, shown in the summer of 1936, was located just south of the Free Bridge.

During Pres. Franklin Delano Roosevelt's Work Projects Administration (WPA) initiative, Phillipsburg began a recreation program. J. Frances Moroney, a Phillipsburg native, was appointed director of this project for Warren, Hunterdon, Morris, and Somerset Counties. The recreation program was approved in Warren County in January 1936. Nicholas Varhall was appointed county supervisor and was given an office in Phillipsburg. In Phillipsburg, a recreation division was formed to conduct indoor programs, which consisted of arts and crafts, physical activities, dancing, quoit games, basketball, minstrel shows, and one-act plays. The recreational division also supervised six playground programs, which offered swimming, softball, stunts, and pet, doll, and baby parades.

On July 11, 1936, William Henry Walters gave Phillipsburg a 24-acre plot of land as a Diamond Jubilee gift. This area was known as Dempster Race Track. Later, the name was changed to Walters' Park. As late as 1961, a footbridge connected Walters' Park and Firth Youth Center. The Phillipsburg Municipal Pool (formerly the Gerry-Mel Pool) is located at Walters' Park.

The Firth Youth Center was a gift from Elizabeth Firth Wade. In 1953, she gave the facility to the city in memory of her father, former mayor Joseph H. Firth. The youth center serves many youth with all type of recreation. In the early 1960s, a basketball court was added to the center.

In 1980, the town opened Delaware River Park along the Delaware River at the rear of Mount Parnassus. There are 23 acres with ball fields, courts, and bike paths, accessible from Howard Street. Phillipsburg has had a lot of sporting programs. Various organizations, such as the firehouses, had baseball and basketball teams.

These youngsters appear to be having a wonderful day at the Phillipsburg Municipal Bathing Beach in the summer of 1936.

One of the events during the Diamond Jubilee year, 1936, was the Brensinger School Costume Parade.

In 1933, Phillipsburg held its first annual Easter Egg Hunt. In 1960, these youngsters are attending the town's 27th annual Easter Egg Hunt.

The Acmon Basketball Team of 1905 included, from left to right, the following members: (front row) Kenneth Smith, Sam Frame, Thomas Brennan, and Walt Wynkoop; (back row) Ernest Barker, Bart Reading, Frank Gill, and Ronald Reed. The team played at Ortygia Hall on Hanover Street.

This football game is being held at the Standard Silk Mill Field in 1911. The players in the striped shirts are members of the Phillipsburg High School team. Today, this site is where the Firth Youth Center is located.

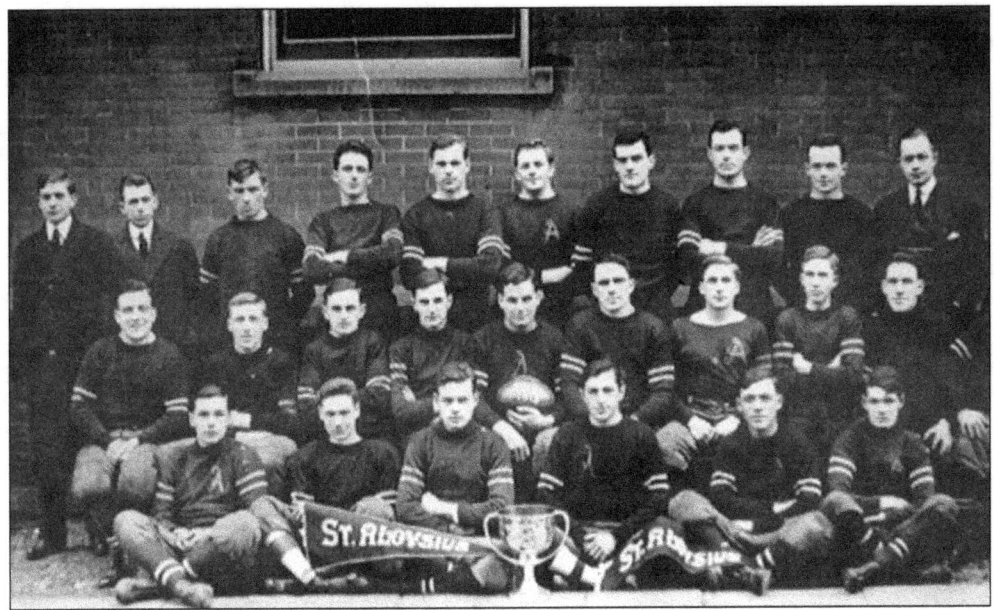

The 1913 Saint Aloysius football team includes, from left to right, the following: (front row) J. Klenney, J. Nixon, R. Flynn, J. Deida, J. Gaghan, and F. Gallagher; (middle row) J. Kelly, H. Pfeiffer, James Smith, Jack Smith, J. Tirrell, T. Halley, R. Brown, V. Reilly, and T. Eurell; (back row) F. Korp, W. Shaneberger, F. Connolly, J. Flynn, A. Rhea, A. McKay, R. Bratch, P. Kelly, W. Gaynor, and J. Morrison.

The Warren Athletic Club baseball team poses in front of the William Harwig School in 1911. Members are, from left to right, as follows: (front row) J. Tucci, J. Gallagher, H. Bowers, and A. Blandis; (back row) B. Boice, D. Elwood, T. Bankosh, P. Osborne, E. Gallagher, Buckey Smith, and Bill Smith.

The Alert Fire Company baseball team of 1885 includes, from left to right, the following: (front row) T. Raub, E. Barnett, and A. DeWitt; (middle row) F. Titus, J. Firth, F. Connolly, H. Edinger, and A. Tallman; (back row) C. Person, F. Mutchler, B. Durling, V. Dull, M. Ryan, and A. Ferguson.

On July 11, 1936, William Henry Walters (left) donated the old Dempster's RaceTrack to the town to create a municipal park. The area is known today as Walters Park.

The Columbia Athletic Club football team of 1903 includes, from left to right, the following: (front row) P. Tirrell, "Goat" Lynch, R. Surran, E. Fisher, and E. Tirrell; (middle row) F. Tirrell, "Shoots" Carpenter, "Mink" Lynch, and E. Connell; (back row) G. Carpenter, "Hook" Felker, "Lassie" Stone, "Hen" Carpenter, M. Storms, and unidentified.

The Standard Silk Mill women's basketball team is shown in 1912.

Among the young people dancing at the Firth Youth Center in 1954 are Peggy Hopewell Butler, front and center, and Ann Bobinis Clasen, left rear, wearing a dark blouse with a white collar.

Playing Pool at the Firth Youth Center in 1954 is Bob Stem, far left.

Phillipsburg High School's first varsity wrestling team is shown in 1947. The team's record that season was zero wins and seven losses.

In 1932, the Chicago White Sox played Phillipsburg's North End team at North End Field, which was located in the Flats. The North End team won 7–6. In the second row are Charlie Berry of Phillipsburg, third from the right, and Frank Grube of Easton, Pennsylvania, second from the right.

The crossing-watchman's shanty was located at the southeast corner of Union Square and South Main Street in front of the Pennsylvania Railroad passenger station. The police officer is Amos "Sparky" Hedden, shown c. 1940.

Eight
Transportation

Ralph Rush uses an early means of transportation along Bennett Street in 1919.

In the early days in Phillipsburg, people traveled by foot, horseback, or buggy. Rafts were used to cross the Delaware River.

One of the first settlers in the area was David Martin. In 1737, Martin was granted permission to run a ferry at the Forks of the Delaware. He had rights to ferry from Tinicum Island in the north to Marble Mountain, in Morris County, in the south. He ran the ferry between Phillipsburg and Easton, Pennsylvania. The early ferry was a canoe, which he paddled back and forth. If his passenger had a horse, the horse had to swim aside or behind the canoe. In 1798, Thomas Bullman, a self-taught physician, bought the rights to Martin's Ferry. He also purchased the area now known as Union Square, as well as land along Main Street.

In 1797, erection of a covered, wooden bridge was begun across the Delaware River, connecting Phillipsburg and Easton. Due to a lack of funds, work stopped until 1805. In 1802, the Sussex Road, which was part of the New Brunswick Turnpike, now North and South Main Street, was completed. The completion of the covered bridge in 1806 was an impetus to the development of Phillipsburg.

In the mid-1860s, the trolley system was begun. The Phillipsburg Horse Car Rail Road Company was chartered on April 9, 1867. The track extended from Union Square to Anderson Furnace. The company operated out of a carbarn and stable on North Main Street just north of Union Square. In 1885, the company expanded into Easton, Pennsylvania. On June 30, 1892, the Easton Transit Company purchased the Phillipsburg Horse Car Railroad Company. On March 10, 1899, the Easton Consolidated Electric Company took over the Phillipsburg Horse Car Rail Road Company. On October 11, 1916, the Easton Transit Company reorganized the Phillipsburg Horse Car Rail Road Company as the Phillipsburg Transit Company. On March 1, 1922, the Lehigh Valley Transit Company took over and made it a part of its company.

The Center Square & Delaware Passenger Railway, a horse-drawn carriage company, was chartered on March 5, 1871. This company was an offshoot of the Phillipsburg Horse Car Rail Road Company. In 1885, it began service over the covered bridge. On June 30, 1892, the Center Square & Delaware Passenger Railway was taken over by the Easton Transit Company.

The Easton & Washington Traction Company was chartered on March 31, 1902. The company constructed an electric railway between Easton and Port Murray via Phillipsburg. The railway followed the Morris Canal between Phillipsburg and Port Murray. The Easton Consolidated Electric Company refused to give the Easton Washington Traction Company operating privileges in Easton. In January 1906, the Easton & Washington Traction Company began service from Lovell Square. On October 16, 1906, service to Port Murray was completed. Because the Easton & Washington Traction Company had no service in Easton, four large automobiles were utilized to transport passengers from Easton to Lovell Square. In 1910, after the Hay family took control, the company's name was changed to the Northampton–Easton & Washington Traction Company. Plans were developed to erect a trolley bridge across the Delaware River, but this failed due to a lack of funds. On April 26, 1923, the company was sold under foreclosure due to bankruptcy. The new owners reorganized under the name of New Jersey Interurban Company. The New Jersey Interurban Company ceased operations on January 27, 1925.

Timothy Palmer planned and built the wooden covered bridge, which opened in 1806. Thomas Bullman sold some of his land in Union Square for the Phillipsburg approach to the bridge. This bridge was a toll bridge for pedestrians, horsemen, and trolley cars. In 1895–1896, the covered bridge was replaced by the present Free Bridge. In 1938, the Bushkill Street Bridge (Focht Bridge) was erected. Today, Route 22 carries a large number of cars and trucks across this bridge daily. *Above:* Depuy's Ferry crosses the Delaware River from Richmond Road in Pennsylvania to Roxburg Station *c.* 1890. *Below:* This is the Union Square entrance to the covered bridge.

On July 2, 1852, the Central Railroad of New Jersey, the first railroad to Phillipsburg, was completed. This event was greeted by the ringing of church bells and an artillery salute from the top of Mount Jefferson in Easton, Pennsylvania. The cities of Phillipsburg and Easton joined in the celebration. There were parades and dinner parties. The Central Railroad of New Jersey discontinued all passenger service in 1967. For a period beginning in 1974, commuter service was extended to Phillipsburg from Newark.

At approximately 1:00 p.m. on February 3, 1854, the Belvidere–Delaware Railroad, on its first run, arrived at Union Square. Aboard were hundreds of prominent businessmen, civic leaders, and local and state political figures. They were greeted by a crowd of several thousand people, who turned out for this big event. As the train approached, cannons were fired, bells were rung, and flags were waved. Festivities continued until 9:30 the next morning. Events included parades, banquets, dances, and speeches. It was not until 1855 that the Belvidere–Delaware Railroad entered Easton over the newly constructed, wooden, double-decker railroad bridge. In 1876, the Pennsylvania Railroad took control of the Belvidere–Delaware Railroad. Daily passenger service from Phillipsburg to Stroudsburg, Pennsylvania, ended in 1947. That service was only available on Sundays. In 1960, the Belvidere–Delaware Railroad ceased all passenger service from Phillipsburg.

In 1889, the Phillipsburg–Easton area was a junction for five major railroads. The citizens of this area were able to go anywhere at anytime. During this period, a minimum of 64 passenger trains per day arrived and departed from the Phillipsburg-Easton area.

A stable of the Phillipsburg Horse Car Rail Road Company was located at 20–24 North Main Street. Shown, from left to right, are blacksmith Will Stout, hostler Milton Weidner, unidentified, horsecar driver Frank Hack, blacksmith Bill Stocker, unidentified, and line superintendent John Houseman.

The Phillipsburg Horse Car Rail Road trolley is shown in front of Edward McHale's Shoe Shop, at 529 South Main Street (now 354-South Main Street), *c.* 1878.

This 1910 photograph was taken at the lower end of South Main Street. In the automobile on the left are John Pursell and Chris Hoffman. Standing is Abe Young, and the motorman is Zach Walters.

Easton Transit Company trolley No. 403 loads at Union Square in 1918.

The Union Station of the Central Railroad of New Jersey and the Delaware, Lackawanna and Western (DL & W) Railroad was at 178 South Main Street. This building was erected in 1912 and was photographed here in 1955. Today, it is the home of Gold Cup Sporting Goods.

Electrified cars of the Phillipsburg Horse Car Rail Road stand in Union Square in 1895. These cars were formerly horse-drawn cars.

The Delaware, Lackawanna and Western Railroad passenger station was near the Market Street crossing. This view dates from c. 1900.

The Delaware, Lackawanna and Western Railroad prided itself on cleanliness. In a white dress, Madelaine Murray poses on a locomotive to represent the cleanliness of the rolling stock and service.

Shown near Market Street c. 1895 are, from left to right, unidentified, Joseph McCormack, Mr. Bartell, William Warrenburg, and John McCormack.

This c. 1938 view shows Lehigh Valley Transit Company buses in Union Square. The Wardell Hotel is in the background.

This view of the flooded Phillipsburg approach to the Free Bridge was taken on August 19, 1955, before the river peaked and the center of the bridge washed away. It was the worst flood recorded in Phillipsburg history. Note the price of gasoline: 21.9¢ per gallon.

Nine
DISASTERS

During the flood of 1895, water flowed over the Lehigh River Dam. In this view Phillipsburg is to the right.

Located at the Forks of the Delaware, Phillipsburg and has seen many floods. There have been 48 recorded on the Delaware River since the first recorded one in 1687. The most serious was on August 19, 1955. The river crested at 43.7 feet above normal level. This was 5.5 feet higher than the flood of October 1903, which had been considered the worst flood. The flood of 1862, one year after the incorporation of Phillipsburg, may have been the worst flood ever but there are no accurate records or buildings with watermarks to prove it.

A flood in 1803 hampered the first attempt to build a bridge connecting Phillipsburg and Easton, Pennsylvania. A wooden covered bridge was completed in 1806 and held up to all the high waters the Delaware had to offer. In 1895–1896, the covered bridge was replaced with the present Free Bridge. The Free Bridge stood up to flooding until August 19, 1955. Hurricane Diane hit the area on August 18, moving north with excessive rain. On August 19, the Delaware River reached its peak and took out the center of the Free Bridge.

The Municipal Bathing Beach was photographed during the flood of 1936.

The Northampton Street Bridge withstood all that Mother Nature sent down the Delaware River for almost 60 years. On August 19, 1955, the bridge gave way, and a lifeline between Phillipsburg and Easton was broken. The bridge is shown after the floodwaters receded. Phillipsburg is in the background.

This is a view of North Main Street looking toward Union Square during the 1903 flood. The water came up from the Delaware River through a viaduct located across from these buildings. Today, elevated land and railroad tracks are located where the viaduct once was.

A group of spectators on the Northampton Street Bridge view the ice chunks floating down the Delaware River during the flood of 1936. Phillipsburg is in the background.

Lehigh Valley Railroad train No. 9, the Black Diamond, derailed at the east end of the Delaware River Bridge on February 12, 1907. The Lehigh Valley Railroad Station is in the left background.

This derailment took place west of Black Dan's Cut in Phillipsburg on April 9, 1912. This shows train No. 39 engine No. 2419 of the Black Diamond.

On September 15, 1912, a Central Railroad of New Jersey locomotive derailed near Market Street.

In 1916, as this trolley attempted to turn from Madison Square, where Lewis and Filmore Streets join, it jumped the track and ran into 36 Heckman Street.

This photograph of the apartment house at 142–144 North Main Street was taken on July 10, 1945. Beginning at 8:00 p.m. on Monday, July 9, 1945, a three-hour torrential downpour dumped 6.2 inches of rain on the area. That evening hundreds of tons of rock and dirt came down the hillside behind the apartment house, demolishing it and causing four deaths. The rainstorm did enormous damage to the area. Other homes were destroyed, roads were washed out, and there was a foot of debris at the toll bridge plaza.

On Wednesday, February 11, 1959, at 2:28 p.m., the worst explosion in the history of the Phillipsburg plant of the Ingersoll-Rand Company occurred. The explosion claimed four lives and injured 35 others.

A plane crashed at Phillipsburg Airport c. 1949, killing five individuals, one of whom was Kerry Phillips, daughter of the airport owner, Ted Phillips. Several years later, Ted Phillips was killed in a plane crash near Belvidere.

One of the more spectacular fires in Phillipsburg was at Denny's Antiques, at 797 South Main Street. All six of Phillipsburg's fire departments answered the call.

The Palm Garden Restaurant fire called out all the Phillipsburg companies, along with companies from Huntington, Alpha, Stewartsville, New Village, Broadway, Asbury, and Bloomsbury.

The worst explosion in the history of the local Ingersoll-Rand Company plant occurred on Wednesday, February 11, 1959, at 2:28 p.m. Four people died, and 35 others suffered injuries.

This is the fire at Denny's Antiques, located at 797 South Main Street. All of Phillipsburg's fire departments responded to the call.

A crash at Phillipsburg Airport (above) took the life of Kerry Phillips c. 1949. In 1967, fire struck the Wardell Hotel in Union Square (left).

A gas main explosion at Columbus Avenue occurred in 1960.

An explosion at 300 Lincoln Street in 1938 caused damaged to a dozen other homes. No cause was ever found.

This is a view looking east on the Morris Turnpike, now Memorial Parkway, in 1924. On the right at the corner of Potts Avenue is Rowe's Texaco Service Station. The price of gas is 16¢ per gallon.

Ten
VIEWS ABOUT TOWN

This is a view looking up Hudson Street from South Main Street c. 1917.

Phillipsburg is divided into several sections. The Flats are along South Main Street from Union Square to Huntington. At one time the public library and town hall were in the Flats. The North End is the area on North Main Street near the toll bridge and the old Baker Chemical Company. Steele Hill is the area north of Green's Bridge. Pursell Hill is near the Phillipsburg Care Center. Firthtown is located around the Firth School and Marshall Street. The housing development along Heckman Street is known as Heckman Terrace. The housing development off Roseberry Street is known as the Annex. Hillcrest is located between Memorial Parkway and Belvidere Road. Hudson Street Hill is the area from Brainerd Street to Lewis Street. Valley View is a development that stretches from Congress Street to the Ingersoll-Rand Company. Delaware Heights is bordered by Carpenterville Road near Green's Bridge to the Delaware River on the southwest.

These homes are located in the section of Phillipsburg that is known as Fairview Heights.

This view of South Main Street was taken looking south from the Lovell Building (city hall) in the 1960s.

Looking north on Chambers Street from Hudson Street, this view dates from 1906.

In this 1911 photograph of Heckman Street at Silk Avenue, Lewis and Filmore Streets are to the left.

This view of South Main Street was taken looking south to Market Street in 1905.

Near the corner of Stockton Street, this view of South Main Street was taken was taken looking north c. 1905.

Looking north from Hudson Street, this view shows Lewis Street in 1908.

This 1900 view shows the approach to the Free Bridge in Union Square.

Hudson Street Hill was also called Tar Walk due to the early, wooden plank sidewalks held together by tar. This 1910 view looks up Hudson Street Hill from Shimer Street.

Glenn Avenue at Schultz Avenue was photographed in 1908.

The removal of the trolley tracks on North Main Street took place in 1937.

This view looks southeast on Warren Street near Anderson Street and dates from April 9, 1928. The tracks of the old Delaware, Lackawanna and Western Railroad cross the culvert. The house on the left, known as the Roseberry House, was erected c. 1787.

East Boulevard in Alpha was photographed in 1925.

Central Avenue in Alpha was photographed c. 1925.

Joseph "Copey" Orchulli, at age 19, was photographed with his first truck in 1950. Out for a ride, he was watching the young women at Frenchtown High School. He became the proprietor of Copey's Market, at 13th and Butler Streets in Easton, Pennsylvania.

Morris "Mace" Bugen poses with his special vehicle in front of his parents' store, at Marshall and Warren Streets, in 1943. He passed away October 30, 1962, at the age of 67.

ACKNOWLEDGMENTS

Thanks go to Ronald Wynkoop Sr., the Easton Library Marks Room staff, the Phillipsburg Library Staff, Rose Allshouse, Nancy Pinter, Joseph "Copey" Orchulli, Carl R. Baxter, the Phillipsburg Emergency Squad, James Allshouse, and the Warren Hospital public relations staff.

BIBLIOGRAPHY

Buscemi Sr., Leonard. *The 2001 Easton, PA-Phillipsburg, NJ Calendar*; 2000.
———.*The 1995 Easton, PA—Phillipsburg, NJ Calendar*; 1994.
———.*The 1994 Easton, PA—Phillipsburg, NJ Calendar*; 1993.
———.*The 1996 Easton, PA—Phillipsburg, NJ Calendar*; 1995.
Condit, Rev. Uzal. *History of Easton, South Easton, Phillipsburg*; 1889.
Henry, M.S. *History of the Lehigh Valley*; 1860.
Phillipsburg High School. *The Karux of the Class of 1947*; 1947.
Wynkoop Sr., Ronald. *The Old Home Town*; 1977.
———.*A Time To Remember*; 1985.
———.*It Seems Like Yesterday*; 1989.
———.*The Golden Years*; 1972.

OTHER MATERIALS USED

American Journal of Progress; 1899.
Easton Daily Express, Industrial edition; 1893.
Free Press, Industrial and Prosperity edition; 1909.
Golden Anniversary and Banquet of the Jersey Hose Fire Company No. 2; 1937.
Historical Program, Charter Jubilee, Phillipsburg, NJ; 1911.
History of Delaware Park Chemical Engine No. 1; 1993.
History of Warren County, NJ; 1929.
Our Soldiers and Sailors; 1941.
Phillipsburg Emergency Squad 50th Anniversary Book; 1986.
Phillipsburg, NJ Centennial Souvenir Booklet; 1961.
Phillipsburg, NJ Diamond Jubilee Program; 1936.
Phillipsburg Our Town Part 1; 1989.
West's Directory of Easton, PA and Phillipsburg, NJ; 1923.

www.ingramcontent.com/pod-product-compliance
Lightning Source LLC
Chambersburg PA
CBHW080905100426
42812CB00007B/2163